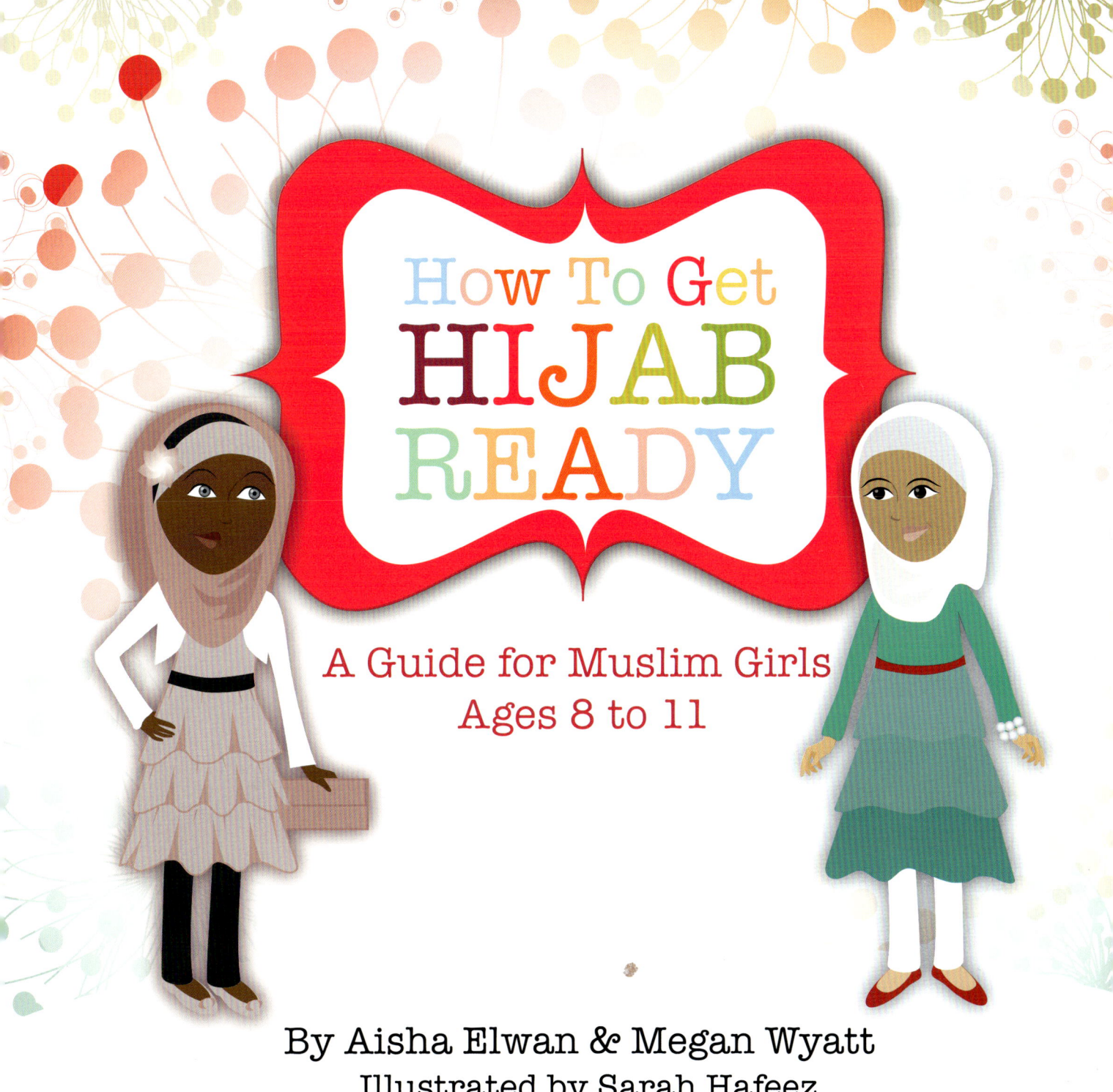

Prolance

www.prolancewriting.com
California, USA

©2014 Aisha Elwan
& Megan Wyatt

ISBN-13: 978-0-9885070-5-0

Printed in USA

All rights reserved. No part of the publication may be reproduced in any form without prior permission from the publisher.

Contents

The Basics
What is hijab & why do Muslim girls wear it?....10
What age do I have to start wearing the hijab?....11
Who can I not wear hijab in front of?....12

Getting Started
What are the requirements of of hijab?....16
So, what should you wear?....17
How & where should I begin practicing?....18
How do I put up my hair when I wear hijab?....20
What kind of hijabs are there?....21
Where do I go shopping for hijab friendly clothes?....22
What should I wear for playing and outdoors?....24
What kinds of outfits work best for a special occasion like Eid or a wedding?....25
How can I dress for school and still fit in?....26
How can I use accessories?....27
How exactly do I put on the hijab?....28
How many different ways can I secure my hijab?....30
What do I wear if I want to go swimming?....31

Having Conversations
What do I tell my Muslim friends?....34
How do I explain hijab to my non-Muslim friends at school?....35
What do I say if a stranger in public asks me why I cover my hair?....36
How do I handle the extra attention from older aunties and uncles at the masjid?....38

Worries & Concerns
What do I do if my hair falls out of my ponytail or bun?....42
Will anything bad happen to my hair if I cover it?....43
What if I take my hijab off later? Am I ready to start now?....45
What if I get made fun of at school?....47

Your Reward for Good Deeds
Will Allah be pleased with me?....50

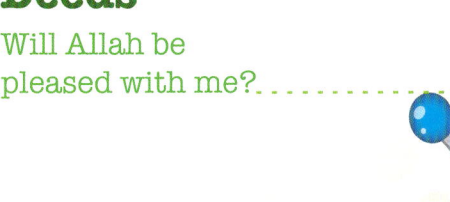

As'salamu Alaikum Parents,

I realize that one of the greatest challenges of my life is raising children, and not just raising them, but aiming to instill in them a love for Allah and His Messenger (saw) and a strong commitment to living Islam. I am pretty sure you agree with me too!

One of the the facets of Islam which our young daughters must commit to is covering according to Islamic guidelines. In short, "wearing hijab," and all that this modern phrase entails. It's one of the aspects of Islam I deeply value, and each day see great wisdom in it's consistent practice for women.

While culture around the world has given many different meanings to "hijab," I pray we can bring our young Muslimahs back to a place where they value what Allah (swt) has said in The Qur'an about covering, and find the honor and dignity it is meant to bestow on them.

In a world heading the opposite direction, it's no easy feat to be a young girl, or even an adult woman, who stands out from the crowd because of her clothing in such an obvious way. It takes courage, commitment, and grace to take on this challenge everyday.

Recognizing this, I believe that we need to give our girls plenty of time to learn about hijab, warm up to it, practice it, and finally, commit to it in a process that is almost seamless, natural, and positive.

Let little girls be little girls. Let them play, romp, climb, jump, swing, hang, twirl, and leap their way through childhood. Starting this process doesn't need to interfere with any of this, and when done gently throughout the years with some of the tips in this book, insha'Allah, covering becomes just another normal part of growing up as a Muslimah.

But also, take time to understand their world, recognize their fears, appreciate the power of peer pressure and peer approval, and give many hours through the years to conversation about covering. No question is a bad question, or wrong question. They are all doorways to learning and loving Islam.

May Allah guide us all in our journey as parents. Ameen.

Sincerely,
Megan Wyatt (Um Aisha)

As'salamu Alaikum Young Muslimah! :)

One night in Ramadan 2012, my Mom and I discussed the idea of making a book about how to get ready to wear the hijab. I had wished there was a book like this for me, with fun illustrations and tips, but all the Islamic books about hijab I had seen already were for much older girls.

So we brainstormed ideas for a book written for younger girls which would be colorful, fun to read, and would actually help you decide how to start wearing hijab.

I, myself, used to practice wearing hijab, such as at the masjid, and then I would take it off when I got home. (It wasn't fard to wear it full time yet!)

This process went on for awhile, until one day, I came back from Qur'an class with my hijab on, and that day I looked in the mirror and looked at myself. From that day forward, I decided I wanted to wear it full time, even if it wasn't required of me yet, alhamdulellah, and I told my Mom.

For many girls, the decision to cover isn't easy, and they need a little extra help! I hope this book inspires and helps you prepare for the day you decide to cover with confidence!

Sincerely,
Aisha Elwan
Age 12 ½

The Basics

What is hijab & why do Muslim girls wear it?

Hijab is a special style of clothing that Muslim girls and women wear because Allah has asked us to do so in The Qur'an.

This style of clothing is usually more modest than what you wear at home, or even what you wear outside the house right now.

In the Qur'an Allah says:

"O Prophet! Tell your wives and your daughters and the women of the believers to draw their veils all over their bodies. That will be better, that they should be known (as free respectable women) so as not to be annoyed. And Allaah is Ever Oft-Forgiving, Most Merciful"

Al- Ahzaab, Ayah 59

There are many books and scholars of Islam who have explained the details on what is required for a Muslim woman when it comes to covering. As you go through this book, we'll be offering those details in a way that's easy to understand insha'Allah!

What age do I have to start wearing the hijab?

This age slightly varies for each girl, but it's based on when your body goes through certain changes that changes you from a little girl into a young lady! Your Mama can tell you more about that. For most girls, however, this usually occurs between the ages of eleven and thirteen.

It's a good idea to start practicing and wearing the hijab and other loose clothing by the time you are ten years old just so you can get used to dressing a little bit differently.

Aisha's Tip!

Don't forget you are still young, so it's ok if your hijab or clothing isn't perfect all the time! After all, girls need to be able to run, jump, climb, swing, and chase friends during playtime. Keep things easy on yourself while you are practicing!

Who can I not wear hijab in front of?

You do not have to cover all the time when you do decide to wear the hijab. For example, if you are around only women and young children, you can wear whatever funky fashion you want along with your favorite hairstyle, make-up, and jewlery.

You also do not have to cover in front of the following males who are mahram to you:

- Your father
- Your brother (if you have any!)
- Your uncles who are related to one of your parents (which means your mother's brother, or your father's brother in case you were confused)
- Your nephews - If you have older siblings who have children, a nephew is their son
- Your grandfather on both your mom and dad's side
- Step-father - if your mother is remarried to someone who is not your own father

Any male not on this list is called a "non-mahram." That includes male cousins that you are related to, family friends that might come by and other male family members.

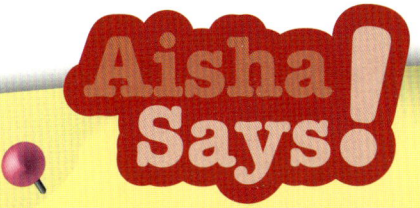

Aisha Says!

Here is how I remember who is a mahram and non-mahram. Your mahram is someone you could never ever marry in the future.

A non-mahram is someone you could marry way waaaay in the future! I know it seems so weird to think about that now, but it's just an easier way to remember who is who, and explain to others who you have to cover in front of!

New Word

A non-Mahram is a phrase that blends English and Arabic together! Non means "not." A "Mahram" means someone that a Muslim female cannot marry. It might sound weird to think of the concept of marriage at our age, but it's the easiest way to explain the meaning! So a non-Mahram is a male who you could technically marry in the future. ☺

Getting Started

What are the requirements of hijab?

Hijab is the nickname we use today to describe two requirements from the Qur'an. In the Qur'an it uses the words *khimaar* and *jilbab*. A khimaar is a headcovering in the Arabic language, and jilbab refers to loose outer clothing.

Some people use the word hijab to only mean the scarf on your head, but this is not a good example, because then they end up covering their hair, but don't follow the guidelines for the rest of their body.

When we use the word hijab, we are talking about both, the head covering, and your clothing.

So, what should you wear?

Clothes should be loose, not see through, and end at your wrists on your arms and ankles on your legs.

Long dresses

Knee length tunics (which means long shirts)

Long skirts

Knee length skirts with cotton leggings underneath

How & where should I begin practicing?

The best place to begin is at home. Let your family members know you are now a "muhajabah in training!" Then, choose a time to practice covering, for example going to the grocery store with your mom, or when you are at the masjid.

Aisha Says!

It's ok to feel happy and proud that you are wearing the hijab in public places.

Afterall, it's a big step for us girls to make.

New Word

Muhajabah is an Arabic word for a girl who is covering her head with the hijab along with modest clothes.

How do I put up my hair when I wear hijab?

There are several different ways you wear your hair under your hijab. If you have long hair try wearing it in a bun.

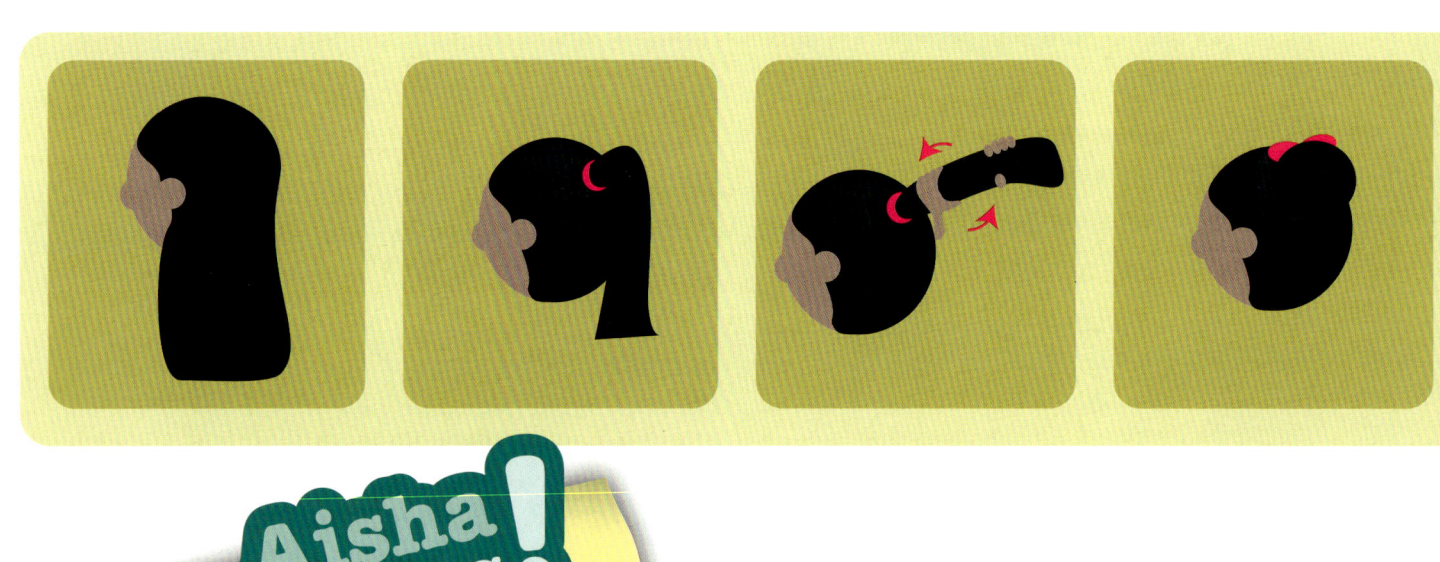

Aisha Says!

Be careful that you don't pull your hair too tight! You might be worried if you don't that your hair might slip out, but it won't if your bun is done properly. I once got a headache wearing my hair too tight!

If you have short hair, you can wear a short ponytail, and if you have bangs, use barrettes to hold the hair back away from your forehead.

Find what is comfortable for you and easy to do on your own everyday. Of course you might need to practice a little bit!

What kind of hijabs are there?

There are many different styles of hijab, and the most popular are usually one of three kinds.

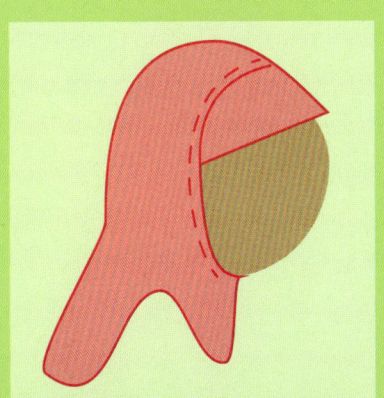

Pull-on hijabs are either one piece or two, which you can simply slide onto your head and go!

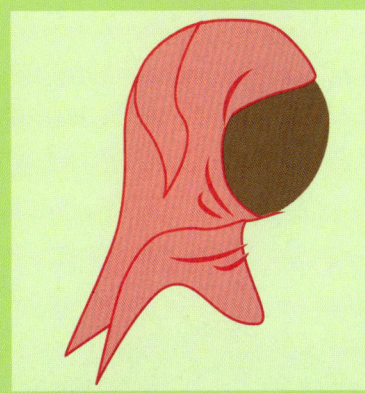

Next, there are square shaped hijabs, which are folded into a triangle before it's pinned around your head.

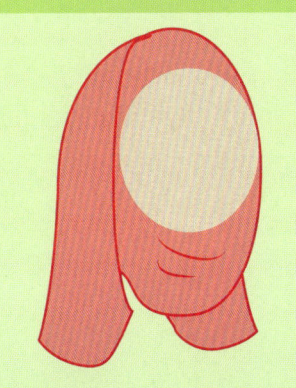

Finally there are rectangles, which can be really long and wide, or shorter and narrow. These are wrapped around your head secured with pins as well.

Aisha Says!

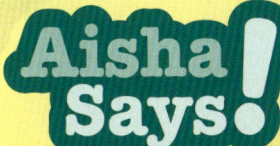

How do you decide which one is right for you? You might need to try all three to decide which kind feels the most comfortable on your head. Right now, I only like pull on hijabs because they are quick, easy, soft, and don't require a lot of time to put on.

There are so many different colors and designs to choose from, it may be hard to pick which ones to buy. A great starting place is to choose a few simple colors that match lots of outfits, for example white, black, cream, and one of your favorite colors. Then you can mix and match with your outfits at home.

Where do I go shopping for hijab friendly clothes?

There is almost always a place you can find clothing to create your hijab friendly wardrobe! In spring and summer, look for long or medium length dresses, light weight cardigans, skirts, and cotton leggings or jeans.

In fall and winter, you can find jumpers, longer jackets, long sleeved t-shirts for layering, and with a bit more layering, you can make your spring/summer garments wearable even in winter!

SPRING & SUMMER

FALL & WINTER

What should I wear for playing and outdoors?

If you are heading to the playground, a soccer game, or a hike, you need to be able to run, jump, skip, leap, crawl, climb, kick, twirl, and any other movement you might do while being active!

These outfits will work best!

Dresses to the knee over pants.
Long sleeved t-shirts, knee length skirts, and pants.

Aisha Says!

When you are playing, like tag or running around, wear knee length dresses because it's easier to run in, and prevents you from tripping and falling, which might happen if you were wearing a long dress or skirt.

What kinds of outfits work best for a special occasion like Eid or a wedding?

Dressing up for Eid or a special event is a wonderful way to enjoy your hijab, because there are so many pretty ways to dress up! Here are some suggestions:

1) Formal long satin dresses with a cardigan leggings, sparkly hijab, pretty shoes and matching handbag.

2) Add pretty hair pins, head bands, or flower clips on your hijab.

Aisha's Tip!

When buying a formal dress, get one a bit bigger than your actual size so it will be longer. If you wear a sweater over it, no one else will notice it's a bigger size, and it's more modest because it fits a bit loosely.

How can I dress for school and still fit in?

Your clothes for school are just a modified version of what you are already wearing. By taking the step to start wearing hijab, to be ready for when it is required, you are going to have to accept that your clothes and style aren't going to look like everyone else at school. And that's OK!

If you look around at school, you'll see that everyone wears what they like too! But your clothes carry a deeper meaning for you, which is truly special.

Here are some "hijab" makeovers of some classic back-to-school looks.

How can I use accessories?

Accessories are so much fun, and allows you to express your own personal style and creativity with your clothes. Here are some hijab friendly ways to do that!

1) Long necklaces that hang over hijab
2) Bracelets
3) Pretty hijab pins
4) Coordinating hijab style with purse/backpack
5) Undercaps with different colors
6) Shoes

How exactly do I put on the hijab?

There are several different styles of hijab to choose from, and each them goes on a little bit differently. Here is a simple step by step to get you started.

Square Hijab

Step 1: Fold in half creating a triangle.

Step 2: Place the folded edge against your forehead, and the rest of the scarf behind your neck.

Step 3: Position on your head with "flaps" hanging over your shoulders.

Step 4: Pin under your chin with a safety pin.

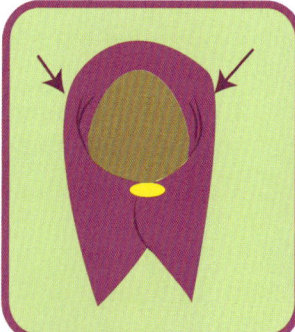

Step 5: Tuck scarf around face so it's snug.

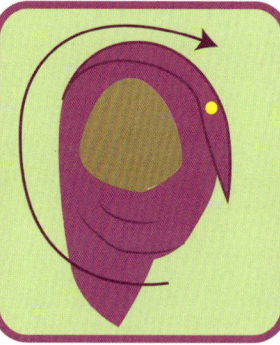

Step 6: Wrap one "flap" under your chin, onto your head, and pin in place.

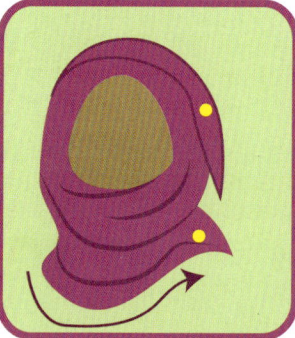

Step 7: Take side of second flap, and pin on your shoulder, covering your chest.

Step 8: Adjust scarf so material is laying neatly and shoulder pin is hidden.

Rectangular Hijab

This is pretty much the same steps as the square hijab, except that there is no folding and triangles. You begin right away with placing the scarf on your head.

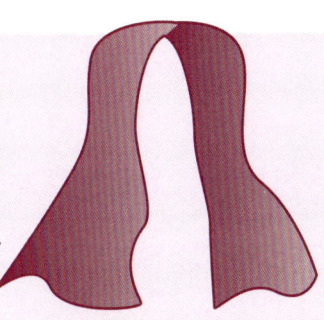

Pull-On

Pull on hijabs are the easiest hijab to start with, because usually no pins are required! You might need a pin under your chin, to gather some of the fabric if the one you bought is made for an adult, so that it won't slip off your head!

Aisha Says!

Try wearing a hijab cap!

A hijab cap helps your hijab from sliding and being see-through. They come in different colors to match your different outfits, but white goes with almost anything! Warning! Some of them are sewn too tightly! If this is the case, and it's too late to return one, you can stretch out the seam with your hands until you hear a little ripping sound. It makes it a little looser, and much more comfortable on your ears!

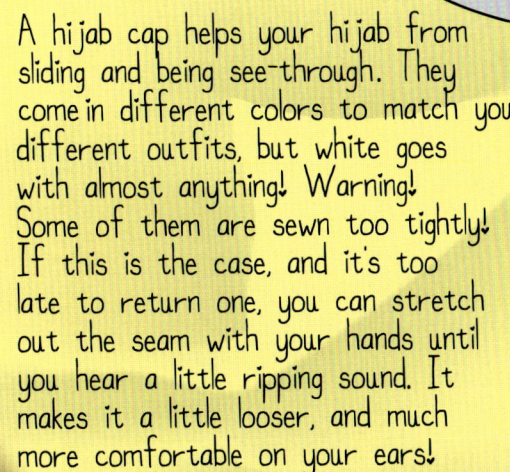

How many different ways can I secure my hijab?

There are different kinds of pins you can use and wear for securing your hijab, which is especially important if you are wearing a square and rectangular hijab.

You can ask your Mama which kinds of pins are best for the fabric you are wearing. Sometimes, a simple safety pin, which you buy easily at a store, will do.

Other times, you need a special pin that doesn't have a circle at the end (like a safety pin) to avoid your hijab material getting a hole and tear in it.

Asking someone a little older and experienced to show these to you makes it easier to understand, and know which ones to choose. No matter which one you choose, be careful when handling pins, as they are sharp!

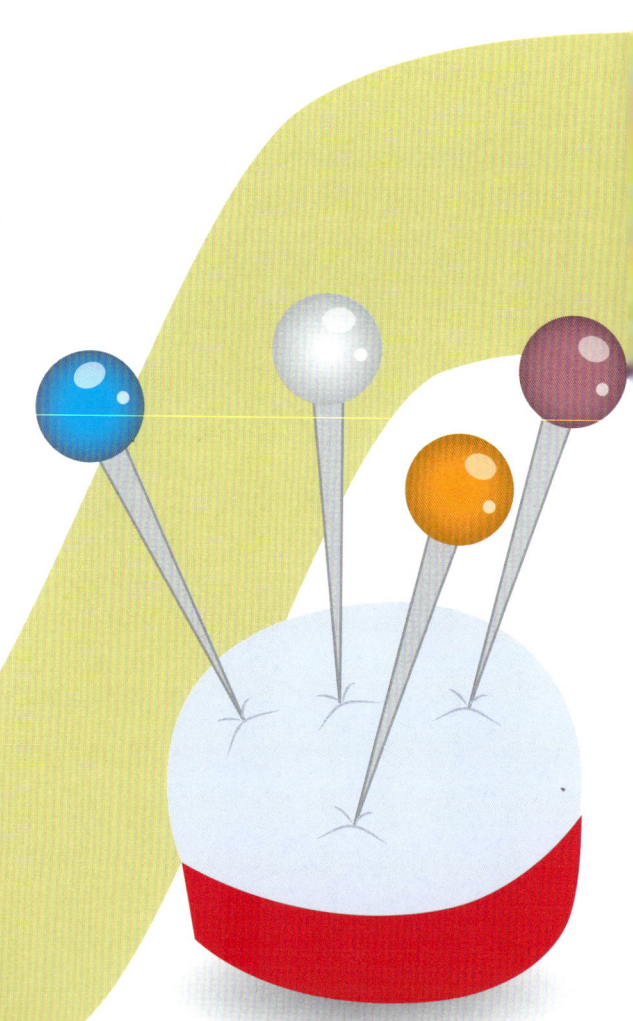

What do I wear if I want to go swimming?

Swimming is a wonderful sport that is really good for your body. Whether you live by a beach or have access to a pool, you can and should still swim!

At your age, it would be ok if you didn't cover while swimming, and chose to wear modest swim clothes instead. Remember, you want to ease into covering at your age, and it can be tough to find hijab friendly clothing for young girls.

Nowadays, there are more and more options available for teens and adults, but maybe not for a girl your age, which is why we don't want to over complicate things!

However, more Muslim girls' swimsuits are becoming available online, which come with water friendly fabrics that keep you covered, so you can ask your parents to help you look.

Here are some other alternatives that are close!

1) Long swim shorts and swim shirts.

2) One-piece sun protection outfits.

3) Waterproof sun hats and visors.

The bonus is that you'll also be protected from the sun, preventing sunburn!

Having Conversations About Hijab

How do I explain hijab to my non-Muslim friends at school?

If you decide to start covering at school, or if a classmate sees you covered somewhere outside of school, you might feel a little embarrassed at first. Your friend is used to you dressing and blending like everyone else, so they may not know how to react to your new style, which could make you feel a little awkward. This feeling will pass, however, as soon as you remind yourself why you are covering now, and that it's to please Allah.

It can help if you tell your friends about the changes yourself, before they have to ask. By taking charge of the conversation, you are also making it easier for them to ask questions.

It would be a good idea to start letting your friends know about your religion, that you are a Muslim, and that someday, you'll be dressing a little bit differently than you are now. After all, if they are really your friends, they'll accept you for who you are.

Aisha Says!

One time, I had to go to take some tests for school, and since I'm homeschooled, that meant meeting up with lots of kids I didn't know. At lunchtime, I saw some girls from my test table, so I decided to join them because I didn't know anyone else. One girl then asked me, "Why do you wear that thing on your head?" And another girl chimed in saying, "yea, why?" Then, a third girl said, "Aren't you hot?" At the time, I didn't exactly know how to answer, but I thought about it and then said, "It's part of my religion and yes I am hot!" After that, everything was fine, but I sure wish I had a book like this to help prepare me for a situation like that.

What do I tell my Muslim friends?

If you are the first amongst your friends to start covering, you may get the reward from Allah for your friends wanting to copy you in something that is good! Just share with them that you've decided to start practicing, and you can even give them a copy of this book to help explain!

Aisha Says!

It's good to let your friends know also, because if they have any older brothers or a father home, your friend can remind you so you can cover up. You may not need or want to cover up yet in front of their brothers or father, but if you do want to practice like that, it's nice to let them know ahead of time.

What do I say if a stranger in public asks me why I cover my hair?

It might happen that a stranger, like at a grocery store, might stop to ask you why do you cover your hair, or what color is your hair. Most people really are just curious to understand why you wear the hijab. A simple and short answer is usually sufficient. For example, you could say, "I wear a head scarf because of my religion. I am a Muslim."

Most people will compliment you on your scarf, or how nice you look in it. A smile and saying thank you is a polite way to receive their well intended compliment.

However, there are some people who may not say something nice because they don't know how to handle people who are different from them. If someone is rude or nasty to you, it is best to avoid speaking back to them. You should tell your parents, and if you are alone, simply walk away. Here is what Allah tells us in The Holy Qur'an about dealing with someone who is ill-mannered:

> "True servants of the Compassionate (Allah) are those who walk on the earth in humility and when the ignorant people address them, they say 'Peace'"
> Al-Furqan, Ayah 63

Humility means to not walk around thinking you are better than anyone else, so that when you do meet someone who doesn't know enough about Islam or what it means to be Muslim, you can either respond with something nice, or since you are young, simply walk away and allow an adult to handle the situation.

How do I handle the extra attention from older aunties and uncles at the masjid?

I go to the masjid with my Baba, and when I was first practicing wearing the hijab there, I got a lot of attention from all of the older uncles. "Oh Habibti, you look so cute," they would say and "Masha'Allah" with big grins on their faces while they surrounded me. I felt weird because I was getting so much extra attention. So I stopped wearing hijab for the rest of the year because I felt so embarrassed being the center of attention. Looking back now, I would tell myself to just be proud of myself for starting to wear the hijab, and that they were just proud of me too."

Aisha Says!

If you are a bit shy, you may need to mentally prepare yourself for a little bit of attention. The adults in your community will be happy so see you making effort to wear the hijab, and some may want to congratulate you, hug you, and even squeeze your cheeks! They see you as their own daughter in a moment like that, and share in the happiness of seeing a young Muslim girl choosing obedience to Allah in her life at such a young age. So, enjoy the positive attention, and simply respond by saying "Alhamdulleh" or "thank you." You'll survive the cheek pinching, we promise!

Worries & Concerns

What do I do if my hair falls out of my ponytail or bun?

Even with your best efforts to secure your hair neatly under your hijab, it can still end up slipping out. It happens to all Muslim women at least a few times! You know how people talk about having bad hair days? Well, we have bad hair and hijab days sometimes! There is no need to panic if this happens. Locate the nearest restroom if you are in public, and ask your parents to take you there if you can't go alone. You can fix your hair there in privacy. If you are are in school, you can request the restroom pass from your teacher.

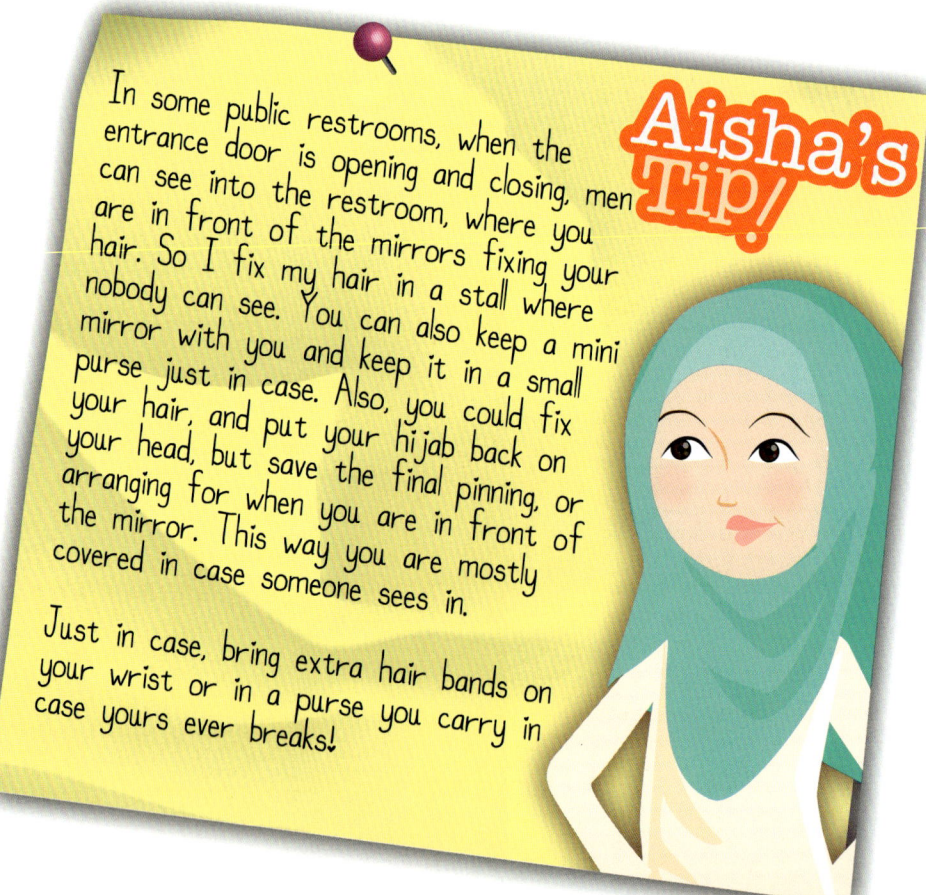

Aisha's Tip!

In some public restrooms, when the entrance door is opening and closing, men can see into the restroom, where you are in front of the mirrors fixing your hair. So I fix my hair in a stall where nobody can see. You can also keep a mini mirror with you and keep it in a small purse just in case. Also, you could fix your hair, and put your hijab back on your head, but save the final pinning, or arranging for when you are in front of the mirror. This way you are mostly covered in case someone sees in.

Just in case, bring extra hair bands on your wrist or in a purse you carry in case yours ever breaks!

Will anything bad happen to my hair if I cover it?

For hundreds of years, Muslim women have been covering their hair with the hijab, and most started out as young girls just like you! They all still have their hair.

While it is true that an existing skin condition on your scalp can be irritated by hijab, the hijab rarely causes the problem. If you notice any significant changes, talk to your parents, and see if you might need to visit a doctor.

One simple recommendation is to not wrap up wet hair often. Take showers in the evening, so your hair can dry, or use a blow dryer to dry up your hair. Having wet hair can also make your hair heavier and pull, which can lead to a headache and a sore head!

You might get a bit itchy and sweaty if you are getting warm, like running around and playing a lot. It helps to experiment with different kinds of fabrics to find out which one you feel best in, like cotton. Save the thicker, less breathable fabrics for colder weather, or special indoor occasions where you won't be running around!

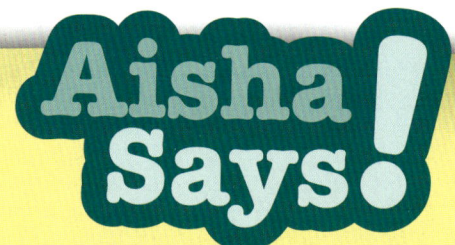

Won't I be hot?

Yes you will be hot in the summer! Everyone is hot in the summer, no matter what they are wearing, but wearing the hijab, it does make things a little bit more steamy. However, remember in the winter, it helps keep you warmer!

One of the main concerns with covering is being too hot! It is true, that the more layers you are wearing, the warmer you might find yourself. However, it helps to choose the right fabrics and thicknesses to help you get through the summer. When it is really hot outside, it is recommended that you stay out of direct sun, stick to shade, and play during the cooler parts of the day. (No matter what you are wearing!)

If you do get light-headed, or over-heated, and feel sick, dizzy, or like you might faint, ask for some help to get some fresh air, a cool sip of water, and relax. Again, most Muslim women, young and old, manage the heat just fine, but if you are sensitive to heat, this may be a bit of an adjustment. Take it day by day, and don't worry that things will always be like this. It will get better and easier as you get used to covering and knowing how your body feels, and when to cool off.

What if I take my hijab off later? Am I ready to start now?

You don't have to start wearing the hijab yet if you are still young, and not yet considered a young woman.

You might even want to wear it right now sometimes, but not all of the time. For example, in the summer you want to go to the swimming pool or beach, and not have to worry about being covered all the way down to your ankles, wrists, and of course your hair.

Maybe you play on a sports team, like a soccer team, or do gymnastics, and you aren't sure about showing up fully covered just yet. If that's the case, then we believe it's better to wear it sometimes, than not at all, so covering starts to become a natural practice in your life gradually.

It's a good idea to spend time around other girls who want to start practicing wearing hijab. This way you can encourage each other and swap style tips!

But what if you are the right age where you are required to cover, or you are younger, and you still want to begin covering full time, but people around you are causing you to doubt your decision?

Here are some examples of things that have been said to other girls similar in age:

"You look so pretty with your nice hair, aren't you going to feel unpretty covering it up?"

"You are too young, why rush a decision like this? It might cause you to miss out on fun things other kids your age are doing. Won't you feel left out?"

"You are going to get made fun of at school, so why put yourself in a situation like that if you don't have to? You can cover when you're much older."

"I am your own mother (sister, aunt, grandmother) and I don't cover, so why should you start covering now? You don't have to if you don't want to."

"People might treat you differently because you look so different from others where we live. How are you going to handle that?"

"If you cover now, you'll get tired of doing it by the time you are a teenager, and you will want to take your hijab off."

All of these statements are not being said to hurt your feelings, or make you angry or worried. They are likely coming from someone who cares about you very much and wants you to be happy, and they are afraid that if you make the decision to cover, that maybe you won't be happy because of it.

Thank anyone who shows concern for you, especially your parents and elder relatives, and see if you can speak to a different elder who does support you in your decision. It can help when other adults speak on your behalf and support you in doing something to please Allah.

If you feel too shy to speak to anyone about how you feel, that's ok too. Insha'Allah, you can try to bring up the conversation again at a future time with someone close to you, until you are ready to wear hijab the way you want in order to please Allah.

What if I get made fun of at school?

Bullying or being made fun of isn't acceptable behavior, and you should never allow someone to put you down, or make you feel bad about yourself. Bullies pick on others to feel powerful because deep down inside they don't feel very good about themselves. When you are being picked on, it's hard to see past their mean personal comments. So here is what we recommend you should do:

1. Tell the bully to please stop speaking like that. A simple comment like "That wasn't very nice" is simple and straight to the point.

2. If it continues or gets worse, speak to your parents and tell them what is going on.

3. Let your parents notify your teacher at school that there is bullying taking place. Usually, a bully isn't only picking on one person at a time. So you will actually be helping out others, and the bully themselves to get some help and stop.

What if you are being picked on or made fun of, but it's from a close friend, neighbor, or relative? The same advice applies. There is never a need to let someone say mean things to you. Walk away from a hurtful conversation, and get support if you need it so things stop permanently. Adults know how to handle these situations best. No matter what someone says to you, even if they try to scare you by telling you something worse will happen to you if you do tell on them, you still need to speak to an adult you trust. This is the right thing to do.

Your Reward for Good Deeds

Will Allah be pleased with me?

Did you know that by choosing to obey Allah in covering, you are earning a lot of reward with Him? There is an angel who writes down all of your good deeds and acts of worship everyday. So everyday, when you are covering and wearing hijab for the sake of Allah, you will have a reward written down for you!

As you grow older, you will find so many reasons to appreciate covering, even if it looks so different from the way many people dress where you live. As time passes, you will be so happy and grateful that you made this decision while you were younger, and blossomed into a young woman already covered beautifully and modestly.

Be proud of who you are, of being a Muslim, and knowing that you have been blessed with a heart that is willing to do what pleases Allah. Here are some verses from the Qur'an talking about the reward that Allah promises for those who believe and worship Him.

"And those who believe and do righteous good deeds, they are dwellers of paradise, they will dwell therein forever."
Surah Al-Baqarah, Ayah 82

"Verily, those who believe, and do deeds of righteousness, their Lord will guide them through their faith; under them will flow rivers in the Gardens of Delight (Paradise)"
Surah Yunus, Ayah 9

"But those who believe and do righteous good deeds, and believe in that which is sent down to Muhammad, for it is the truth from their Lord - He will expiate from them their sins, and will make good their state.
Surah Muhammad, Ayah 2

Be proud of who you are, of being a Muslim, and knowing that you have been blessed with a heart that is willing to do what pleases Allah.